BIG FEELINGS
FEELING ANGRY

by Mary Lindeen

NORWOOD HOUSE PRESS

DEAR CAREGIVER, The *Beginning to Read* Big Feelings books support children's social and emotional learning (SEL). SEL has been proven to promote not only the development of self-awareness, responsibility, and positive relationships but also academic achievement.

Current research reveals that the part of the brain that manages emotion is directly connected to the part of the brain that is used in cognitive tasks such as problem solving, logic, reasoning, and critical thinking—all of which are at the heart of learning.

SEL is also directly linked to what are referred to as 21st Century Skills: collaboration, communication, creativity, and critical thinking. The books included in this SEL series offer an early start to help children build the competencies they need for success in school and life.

In each of these books, young children will learn how to recognize, name, and manage their own feelings while learning that everyone shares the same emotions. This helps them develop social competencies that will benefit them in their relationships with others, which in turn contributes to their success in school. As they read, children will also practice early reading skills by reading sight words and content vocabulary.

The reinforcements in the back of each book will help you determine how well your child understands the concepts in the book, provide different ideas for your child to practice fluency, and suggest books and websites for additional reading.

The most important part of the reading experience with these books—and all others—is for your child to have fun and enjoy reading and learning!

Sincerely,

Mary Lindeen

Mary Lindeen, Author

Norwood House Press
For more information about Norwood House Press please visit our website at www.norwoodhousepress.com or call 866-565-2900.
© 2022 Norwood House Press. Beginning-to-Read™ is a trademark of Norwood House Press.
All rights reserved. No part of this book may be reproduced or utilized in any form or
by any means without written permission from the publisher.

Editor: Judy Kentor Schmauss   **Designer:** Sara Radka

Photo Credits: Getty Images: AzmanL, 29, Flashpop, 26, JGI/Jamie Grill, 3, 14, kdshutterman, 18, leungchopan, 4, Matt Carr, 5, mrs, 6, Noel Hendrickson, 21, PeopleImages, 5, Soren Hald, 22, Stockbyte, 10, Sue Barr, 17, Tom Werner, 25, Westend61, 4, Yasser Chalid, 5, zdravinjo, cover, 1; Shutterstock: all_about_people, 13, PR Image Factory, 9

Library of Congress Cataloging-in-Publication Data has been filed and is available at catalog.loc.gov

Library ISBN: 978-1-68450-820-4   Paperback ISBN: 978-1-68404-668-3

Feeling angry does not feel very good.

But everyone feels angry sometimes.

You might feel angry when something breaks.

You might feel angry if you don't get to do what you want to do.

You might feel angry when someone else takes something you wanted to have.

When you feel angry, you might breathe faster.

Or your face might feel hot.

You might even cry or stomp your feet.

It's okay to let your feelings show.

It can help you feel better.

But sometimes people hit or break things when they feel angry.

Or they bite or kick.

That's not okay.

It's never okay to hurt other people when you feel angry.

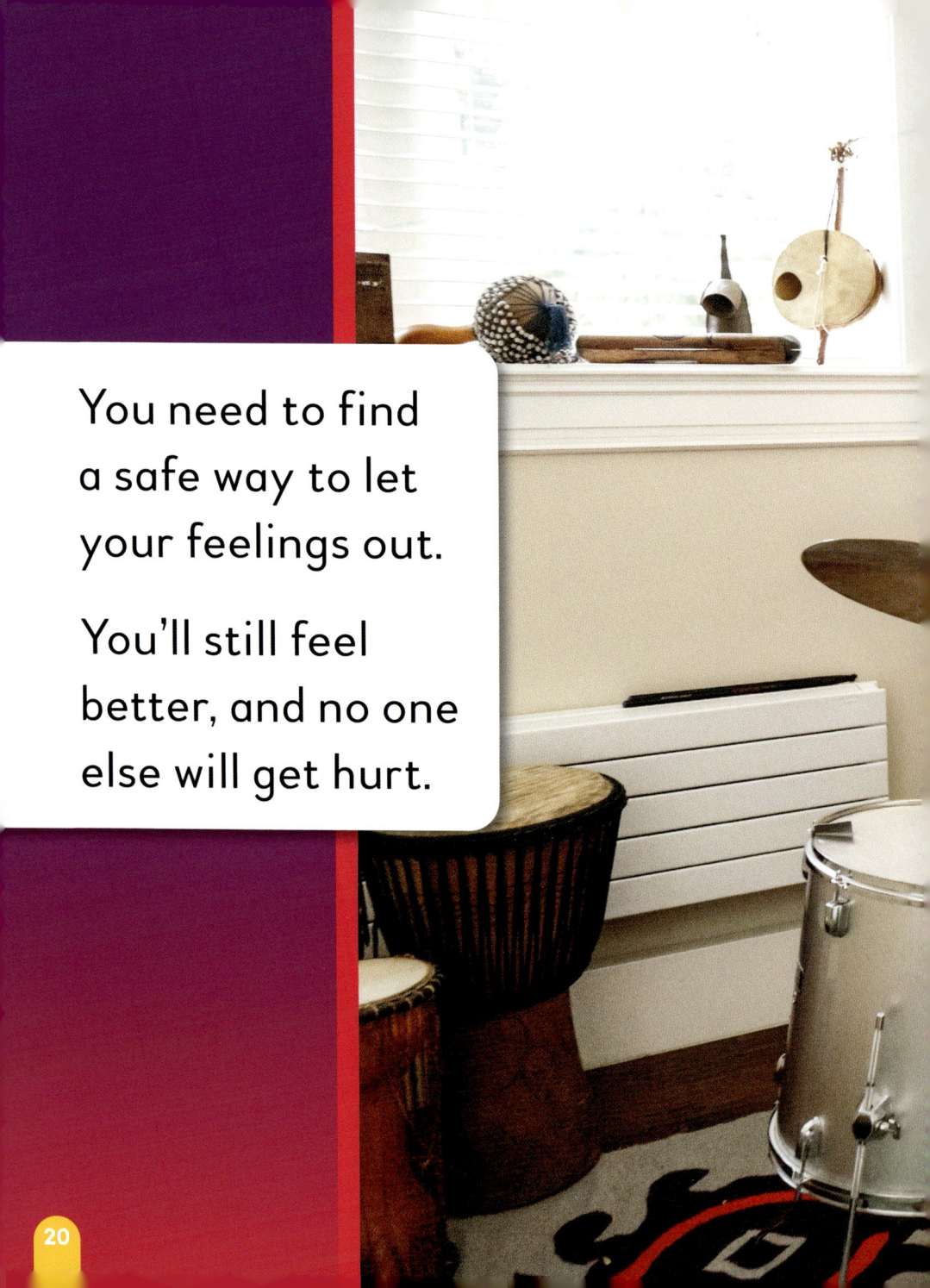

You need to find a safe way to let your feelings out.

You'll still feel better, and no one else will get hurt.

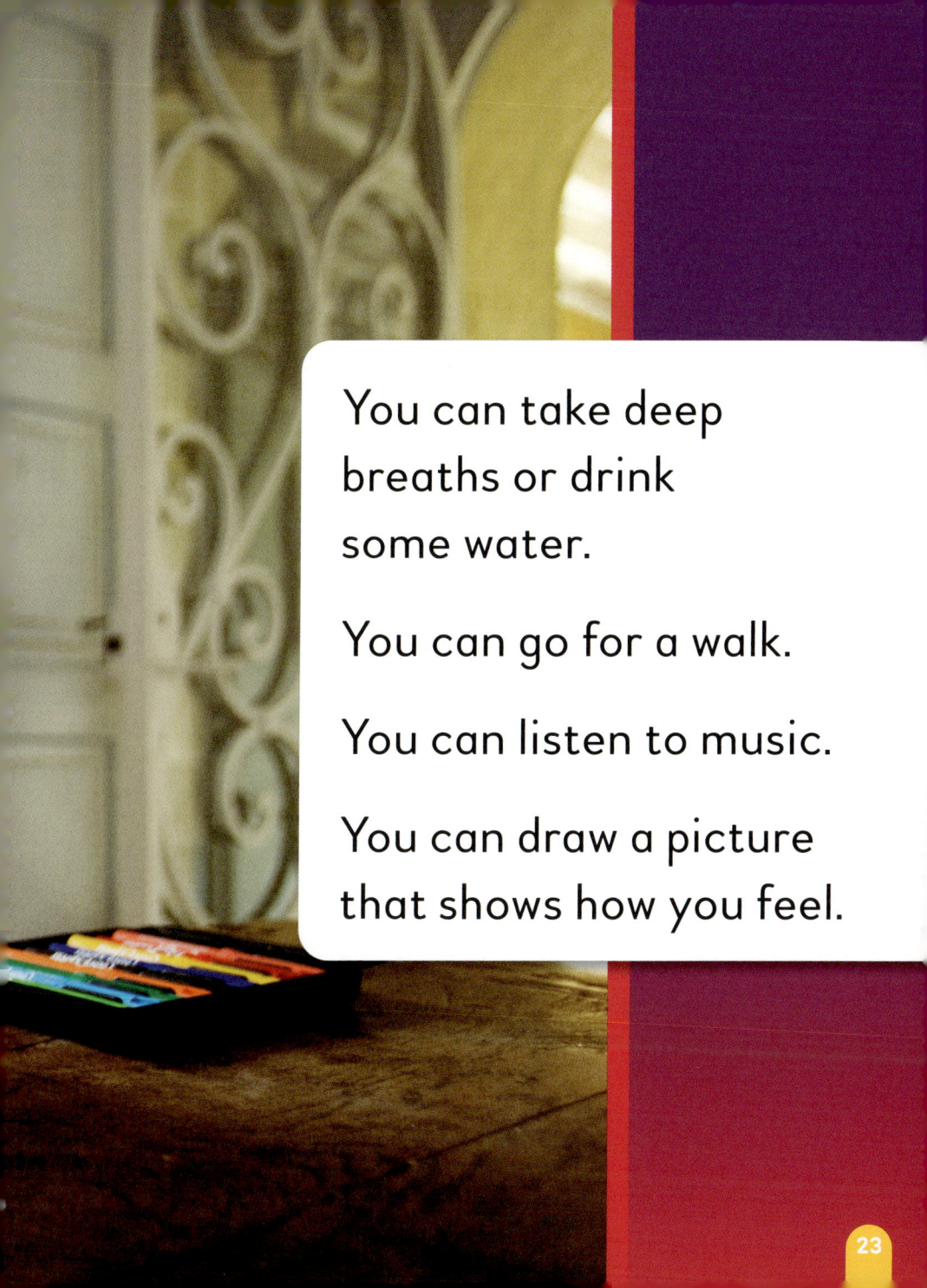

You can take deep
breaths or drink
some water.

You can go for a walk.

You can listen to music.

You can draw a picture
that shows how you feel.

Or you can talk to someone you trust.

When you feel calm, you'll feel better.

And then maybe you'll be able to fix whatever the problem was to begin with.

That will help everyone feel better!

. . . READING REINFORCEMENT. . .

CONNECTING CONCEPTS

CLOSE READING OF NONFICTION TEXT

Close reading helps children comprehend text. It includes reading a text, discussing it with others, and answering questions about it. Use these questions to discuss this book with your child:

1. What does it mean to feel angry?

2. What are some safe ways to let angry feelings out in order to feel better?

Once you have discussed the above questions, ask your child to either draw a picture of someone who is feeling angry or choose one of the children pictured in the book. Then ask the following questions about the child in the drawing or the photo:

1. How can you tell this person might be feeling angry?

2. What might be one reason this person is feeling angry?

3. How would you feel in that situation?

4. Do you ever feel angry? When?

5. When you feel angry, what do you do? How could someone else help you when you're feeling angry?

VOCABULARY AND LANGUAGE SKILLS

As you read the book with your child, make sure he or she understands the vocabulary used. Point to key words and talk about what they mean. Encourage children to sound out new words or to read the familiar words around an unfamiliar word for help reading new words.

FLUENCY

Help your child practice fluency by using one or more of the following activities:

1. Reread the book to your child at least two times while he or she uses a finger to track each word as it is read.

2. Read a line of the book, then reread it as your child reads along with you.

3. Ask your child to go back through the book and read the words he or she knows.

4. Have your child practice reading the book several times to improve accuracy, rate, and expression.

FURTHER READING FOR KIDS

Chien Chow Chine, Aurélie. *Little Unicorn Is Angry*. New York, NY: Little, Brown, and Company, 2019.

Graves, Sue. *I Hate Everything!* Minneapolis, MN: Free Spirit Publishing, 2013.

Krohn, Amy. *My Friend Angry*. Edina, MN: Beaver's Pond Press, 2020.

FURTHER READING FOR TEACHERS/CAREGIVERS

Coping Skills for Kids: Helping Kids Manage Anger
https://copingskillsforkids.com/managing-anger

KidsHealth: Taming Tempers
https://kidshealth.org/en/parents/temper.html?ref=search#catfeelings

Parenting Place: How to explain anger to kids and teens
https://parentingplace.nz/behaviour-and-discpline/help-your-kids-make-sense-of-anger-part-1/

Word List

Feeling Angry uses the 93 words listed below. *High-frequency* words are those words that are used mos: often in the English language. They are sometimes referred to as sight words because children need to lear to recognize them automatically when they read. *Content* words are any words specific to a particulc topic. Regular practice reading these words will enhance your child's ability to read with greater fluenc and comprehension.

HIGH-FREQUENCY WORDS

a	good	other	to
and	have	out	very
be	help	people	want(ed)
but	how	show(s)	was
can	if	some	water
do	it	something	way
does	might	take(s)	what
even	never	that	when
find	no	the	will
for	not	then	with
get	one	they	you
go	or	things	your

CONTENT WORDS

able	draw	it's	sometimes
angry	drink	kick	still
begin	else	let	stomp
better	everyone	listen	talk
bite	face	maybe	that's
break(s)	faster	music	trust
breathe	feel(ing, ings, s)	need	walk
breaths	feet	okay	whatever
calm	fix	picture	you'll
cry	hit	problem	
deep	hot	safe	
don't	hurt	someone	

About the Author

Mary Lindeen is a writer, editor, parent, and former elementary school teacher. She has written more than 100 books for children and edited many more. She specializes in early literacy instruction and books for young readers, especially nonfiction.